EXPRESS YOURSELF

poetry Pt today

EXPRESS YOURSELF

Natalie Nightingale

First published in Great Britain in 2002 by Poetry
Today, an imprint of
Penhaligon Page Ltd, Remus House,Coltsfoot Drive,
Woodston, Peterborough. PE2 9JX

© Copyright Contributors 2002

All rights reserved. No part of this publication may be
reproduced, stored in a retrieval system, or transmitted
in any form or by any means, without prior permission
from the author(s).

A Catalogue record for this book is available from the
British Library

ISBN 1 86226 700 6

Typesetting and layout, Penhaligon Page Ltd, England.
Printed and bound by Forward Press Ltd, England

Foreword

Express Yourself is a compilation of poetry, featuring some of our finest poets. This book gives an insight into the essence of modern living and deals with the reality of life today. We think we have created an anthology with a universal appeal.

There are many technical aspects to the writing of poetry and *Express Yourself* contains free verse and examples of more structured work from a wealth of talented poets.

Poetry is a coat of many colours. Today's poets write in a limitless array of styles: traditional rhyming poetry is as alive and kicking today as modern free verse. Language ranges from easily accessible to intricate and elusive.

Poems have a lot to offer in our fast-paced 'instant' world. Reading poems gives us an opportunity to sit back and explore ourselves and the world around us.

Contents

What Is It Good For?	Don Dolby	1
Blue Moon	Kevin P S Collins	2
Haiku: The Birds	Delia Marheineke	3
Yesterday (By The Beatles)	Mike Proctor	4
Haiku	Marilyn Ashcroft	6
My Song Goes To The Tune Of 'Drink To Me Only'	Len Paget	7
My Heart Is Broken	Pauline Mayoh-Wild	8
Haiku!	Geoff Bookyhead	9
Love Of Life	Alma Montgomery Frank	10
Haiku!	Gemma Stothard	11
Stormy December And Stormy Marriage	Marjorie Cowan	12
Haiku	Angus Richmond	13
HRH The Queen Mother	Gwyneth Elizabeth Scott	14
Haiku	Stan Radcliffe	15
Roll Out The Ballad	B Clark	16
Haiku	Geraldine Laker	17
Hound For Sale	John Pegg	18
Haiku	Sheila M Macmillan	19
Untitled	Winifred Brasenell	20
Haiku	Kath Watkinson	21
Blighty	James Leonard Clough	22
Untitled	I Spencer	23
Haiku	Betsy Williams	24
Slimmer's Lament	Barbara E Martin	25
Haiku	Pleione Tooley	26
Let's Raise A Cheer	Roma Davies	27
Sam	F Jones	28
Just Deserts	R D Hiscoke	29
Haiku	John H Hope	30
Now They're Teetotelin . . .	R Wiltshire	31
Example Of Haiku	Neil A Forrester	32
Untitled	Barbara Goode	33
Haiku	S R Green	34

Salome's Request Granted	Marguerite A Auton	35
Birth	Sue Colson	36
Haiku	Frances Searle	37
Woke Up This Morning With Ye Larke	Norah Morley-Koyich	38
My Song	Nan W Downs	40
Haiku	Sylvia Berwick	41
Wouldn't Start	Wenn The Penn	42
Haiku	Elizabeth Wilson	43
Super Bob Taylor	John Hogan	44
Haiku	Kathy Rawstron	45
I Still Think Of You	Eileen Kyte	46
Haikus	Mary Joseph	47
All For Love	Owen Edwards	48
Haiku	Angela Henderson	49
Untitled	Greta E Bray	50
Someone Special - Me!	Kathryn M Carter	51
From Whom No Secrets Are Hid	D Howard	52
Haiku	J Buksh	53
Mum And Dad	L Berry	54
Haikus	Louise Lee	55
Haiku	John A Mills	56
A Picnic - Through The Looking Glass	Joyce Metcalfe	57
Haikus	Jack Scrafton	58
Make A Change	Valerie Gaynor	59
Haiku	Emelie Buckner	60
Words And Music	Monica Docherty	61
Haiku	Alf Godman	62
Haiku	M Sleeboom-Derbyshire	63
Reflections	Donna Deen	64
A Woman's Work	Anne Gray	66
Haikus	Bella Carroll	67
Haiku	Roger Mather	68
Haiku	Freda Grieve	69
Malfunction	Ann G Wallace	70
Haiku	Monica D Buxton	72
The Unfolding Of Spring	Margaret Kinshott	73

Title	Author	Page
Haikus	Kaz	74
Breakaway Blues	Mary Halfpenny	75
Foreshore	Maureen Oglesby	76
Haiku	S Phillips	77
Haiku	B Lamus	78
The Power Called Love	Tom Usher	79
Haiku	Joan Tompkins	80
Newborn	Faith Bissett	81
Held So Dear	Malcolm Peter Mansfield	82
Whatever	Joan Rea	84
Haiku	Chris Moat	85
Just One More Blessing	Joan Smith	86
Haiku	N D Ifould	87
Untitled	S G White	88
Haiku	Joshua Blanchard Lewis	89
Haiku	Moon Stone	90
Untitled	I T Hoggan	91
Haiku	Sheryl Williamson	92
Dirty White Pickup - The CTRL Test-Pits Song	R D Gardner	93
Haiku	Fuchsia Coles	94
The Best Of Seasons	Meg Phillips	95
My Home	Mary McLeod	96
The Irish Sing-Along	Jean P McGovern	98
Haiku	Sarah Allison	99
Distraction	Pamela Sanders	100
Haiku	Jean Rosemary Regan	101
Help	Archie Livingstone	102
Japanese Haiku	Kathleen M Hatton	103
A Pig's Tale	H Phillips	104
Floral Tributes	Beryl Johnson	105
Shady Stan	E A Triggs	106
Flowering Haiku	Barbara Fosh	107
Parody On Goodbye	Lionel J Nokes	108
Haiku	Tony Meaney	109
The White Cliffs Of Dover	Clare Collins	110
Haiku	Guy Fletcher	111
Hay Fever	Norman Bissett	112

Untitled	Beryl Adamsbaum	113
Shanty In Old Shanty Town	Lincoln Allen	114
Summer Haiku	Chris Creedon	115
Young Swinger	Keith L Powell	116
Loving Lord Jesus	Dennis Brockelbank	117
Untitled	A Whyte	118
Haiku	Anne Greenhow	119
Golden Jubilee	Susan Sissons	120
Haiku	Angela Pritchard	121
Among Our Souvenirs	Sarah Buchan Anderson	122
Along The Grantham Canal	R L Cooper	123
Drink To Me Only	John K Coleridge	124
Haiku	Michael Monaghan	125
Now	Bernadette Leary	126
Haiku	Elizabeth Ellis	127
Wok Of Ages	T W Denis Constance	128
Haiku	Mary McPhee	129
Realism	Beatrice Newman	130
Haiku	Frank Casey	131
Sometimes When We Touch	J Baird	132
Haikus	Charlene Soan	134
Haiku	Kath Gabbitas	135
Haiku	Peter Morriss	136
Haiku	Olwen Way	137
Haiku	David Bowers	138
Haiku	Marcelle Williams	139
Haiku	William Dyer	140
Haiku	Andrew Detheridge	141

What Is It Good For?

Kestrel still above
Eyes alert it swoops to catch
Mouse on ground below.

Blue sky, black dots, bombs
People falling down and down
Quiet now, all dead.

Black night, moon and stars
Are not shining bright tonight
Never to return.

Sun shines, empty fields
Something missing, gone away
Sun shines, no one there.

Leave it to the birds
Lions, tigers hunt in peace
Task of war is done.

Don Dolby

Blue Moon
(To the tune of 'Green Willow' by Foster and Allen)

The blue moon above, shines down on me,
Embracing close, under the blossom tree.
Stars are shining in the night sky above,
True love like ours, from heaven above.
The smell of flowers coming from the glen,
As we kiss my heart beats faster again.
Birds of the air sleep in their nests,
I truly love the one who is the best.
In the distance, lights from a cabin glow,
Our lips meet under a bright starry show.
Sounds of the hounds break the night,
You're such a beauty to this man's sight.
I pledge this heart to you alone,
One day we'll have a cabin of our own.
Who in this world could take your place?
An angel like you, so full of grace.
Take this heart to call your very own,
Love and happiness will fill our home.
Give me the love from your tender heart,
To love forever and never to part.

The blue moon above shines down on me,
Embracing close under the blossom tree.
Stars are shining in the night sky above,
True love like ours from the heaven of love.

Kevin P S Collins

Haiku: The Birds

Collared doves coo down
our chimney pot, while Peter
pots black on TV!

Time out is lost for
'birds of a feather'; thank God,
two now: RIP.

Find binoculars:
Damn! The bird has flown. Quick! Fetch
the RSPB.

Delia Marheineke

Yesterday (By The Beatles)
(Updated version)

Yesterday, all my troubles seemed to be no pay,
Now if Blair and Brown are here to stay,
It might as well be yesterday.

Suddenly, Blair's got cameras watching over me,
Better drive as though I'm 93,
Or my licence is history.

I've done nothing wrong but I know they'll make me pay,
'Cos Blair and Brown screw you each and every way.

What's this spin? It's just lying with a cheesy grin,
Don't believe a word - I won't give in,
Oh I believe in honesty.

Robbed by stealth? It's supposed to save the National Health,
But Brown is sure to stash it all away,
He'll never lose the queues - no way.

I've done nothing wrong but I know they'll make me pay,
'Cos Blair and Brown screw you each and every way.

Tony's flight, meeting 'Dubya' to arrange a fight,
Nuke 'em all and then we'll say goodnight,
Or have you tried diplomacy?

Tony's Dome, big, round garage - give a car a home,
Didn't work out how he planned, you see,
Our Tony's 'place in history'.

I've done nothing wrong but I know they'll make me pay,
'Cos Blair and Brown screw you each and every way.

Yesterday, Blair had morals, now they're thrown away,
Lying every single word he says,
Oh I believe in yesterday.

Mm mm mm mm mm mm mm.

    Mike Proctor

Haiku

Discarded cuttings
Dumped in a forgotten pot
Blooming beautiful

Sunlight and rainbows
Kaleidoscope of colour
Dancing on a dream

Glittering raindrops
Outline a spider's weaving
Priceless masterpiece.

Marilyn Ashcroft

My Song Goes To The Tune Of 'Drink To Me Only'

Speak your love to me with your eyes,
And my lips will tell you mine,
Speak your love to me with your eyes
And let our arms entwine,
Our love will be so sweet and so fair,
Sweeter than the flowers that grow everywhere,
So speak your love to me with your eyes,
And I will always be there,
Speak your love to me with your eyes,
And I will love you forever.

Len Paget

My Heart Is Broken
(To the tune of 'Danny Boy')

My heart is broke because our love is over
The thoughts of you are always in my mind

I miss you so, I wish that you'd come back again
'Cos I'm so sad and feeling so much pain

You are the one I want to spend my future with
I cannot live without you by my side

So please come back and let me prove my love for you
What's done is done, we can't turn back the tide

We had a love that only few could ever know
A love so rare as any love could be

So please come back and say that we can love again
And with your love the pain will go away

My love, my love, I cannot live another day
I need your love, there is no other way

Say you'll be mine for ever and for ever
Because my love belongs to you alone.

Pauline Mayoh-Wild

Haiku!

I cut myself here
To feel the pain that grips me
I feel so useless

Whilst I sit alone
I think of you and me, is
This the same for you?

I went out and you
Were there! Thought you were nice
I was such a fool.

What am I doing
Missing friends so far away
Will I see them soon?

When I'm with you, my
Life seems worth living, you are
My life, I love you.

Geoff Bookyhead

Love Of Life
(To the tune of 'When The Saints Come Marching In')

Love of life, will bring you joy
Love of life will be a toy
For you know what love can bring you
Love of life is ever new.

   Alma Montgomery Frank

Haiku!

I see a vision
Of you, reflected in glass
Is it real? I wish.

I want you to know
How I really am feeling
But cannot, sorry.

I keep trying but
I can't get through, all I want
Is to talk to you.

When I am with you
It is wonderful, I feel
So alive, thank you.

Gemma Stothard

Stormy December And Stormy Marriage
(To the tune of 'Jealousy')

Join me
In my utter misery,
I caused you many a hurt and a tear
Now I want you back my dear.

   Marjorie Cowan

Haiku

To the labyrinth
of a frightened soul that's lost
pray open the door!

Do not mock your priest
Listen at the very least
to the ancient lore

Woman's so worthy
The wise man hoards his money
At her sacred feet

Time waits for no man.
Tide is fickle out of sight
Waiting for time's bite

The rose blooms in spring
Our thoughts begin to shimmer
Our hearts to wander.

Angus Richmond

HRH The Queen Mother
(To the tune of 'Silver Threads Among The Gold')

I recall the Coronation
Then aged five, in '37
Recall a street party
To commemorate it then.
I recall your trepidation
In the East End during the blitz,
For your courage and dedication
Ma'am, you will be sadly missed.

Gwyneth Elizabeth Scott

Haiku

The party was great,
Chatting and drinking for hours.
Their names elude me.

Girl behind the bar
Calls with alluring appeal;
'You forgot your change.'

Raindrops in autumn
Coursing down channelled windows:
Tears for time now gone.

Stan Radcliffe

Roll Out The Ballad
(To the tune of 'Roll Out The Barrel')

I have got bronchitis
Well! Winter's here that's why.
Still I'll get used to it
And I'm not one to cry.
It will soon be summer
So It's off on holiday for us,
With the grandchildren,
In our special family bus!

B Clark

Haiku

autumn's tapestry
tranquil moments - direct from
the stitcher's workbox

fiery fingers of
setting sun rapidly rub
away the day's blue

how sweet the perfume
to inhale for the first time
and to be entranced

    Geraldine Laker

Hound For Sale

With the only hound on this rainy street.
Follow the steady plod, with my aching feet.
As he ever onward trots.
I wish he'd stop.

When the rain so long has been falling down.

In a loathsome way,
On this cussed hound.
He onward pounds.
Hound for sale.

Uncompromising old hound for sale.
Bloodhound, good hound
Onward bounds this dumb hound,
A hound that's only slightly spoilt.
Hound for sale.

Who would like to feel my despair?
Just follow me, I'll take you there.
Hound for sale.

John Pegg

Haiku

Magnolias bloom
Welcoming the morning sun;
Life-giving and warm.

Hospice care so fine,
Touches with love, hope and cheer,
All who venture there.

    Sheila M Macmillan

Untitled
(To the tune 'It's A Long Way To Tipperary')

It's so lovely to be together
And join with our friends.
Enjoying a lovely sing-a-long
With voices loud and strong.
We are the over-sixties
And thank our Lord above
Put our hands together
Give thanks for His love.

Winifred Brasenell

Haiku

Seasonal Beauty

Enjoy each season
aesthetically for its
own special beauty.

The Rainbow

Rain and sunshine meet
in colourful harmony
as the storm subsides.

A Fact Of Life

Yesterday has passed:
Tomorrow is yet to come:
Today be happy.

Kath Watkinson

Blighty
(To the tune 'Camptown Races')

From Romans, Normans, Gaul began,
Carefree townee;
The blending of fine Englishman,
Oh jolly gay.
From painted Picts grew a super breed,
Buckshee grandee.
United Kingdom onwards proceed,
Wiser each day.

Chorus

John Bull eats beefsteak
Likes to have free press.
In dining cars revels in griddle cake,
Somebody has watercress.

James Leonard Clough

Untitled
(To the tune of 'Auld Lang Syne')

My thanks to you Alexander Bell
For inventing that cheerful 'ring'.
A sound of hope in loneliness
The contact that it can bring.
I know it can bring bad news too
But a voice can ease the pain.
Promising to be there for you
Until the sun shines once again.
But - Oh the joy of glad - good news
Brought right into my home
An engagement . . . a wedding - a new baby too.
In whatever order they came
And if I'm really, really low,
And friends are all engaged,
Just needing to hear a human voice
I ring the talking clock again.
Teletext and Intercom are way above my head
But hearing a voice - may from the past
Assures me that I'm not dead.
So thanks to you Alexander Bell
May the ringing never end
For if I was forced to read my messages
I'd just go round the bend.

I Spencer

Haiku

Mouse

Diminutive mouse
Grey, sharp face with alert eyes
Tum, big as a house.

Stream

Mountain stream gurgles
Sparkling waves tumble softly
Small fish dart freely.

Schoolboy

Schoolboy rushes home
Cap askew, red, dirty knees
Happy, free, hungry.

Betsy Williams

Slimmer's Lament
(To the tune of 'Waltzing Matilda')

I've been indulging, I've been indulging,
And now I am bulging, as you'll plainly see,
So I need to be going, shopping for a larger size,
There is more of me than there ought to be.

I am a sinner, I am a sinner,
And I must get thinner, that's easy to say,
But the cake shops are tempting, breaking down my new resolve,
Must walk away, and have no cakes today.

I have been dreaming, I have been dreaming,
And I woke up screaming, as you must have heard,
For I dreamt that you told me, that we were through
                                        because I'm fat,
That's quite absurd, I just eat like a bird.

Who am I kidding? Who am I kidding?
I will do your bidding, I know I must choose,
So I'll have to be cutting down, on all the food that I enjoy,
Weight I must lose, or it's back to the booze.

    Barbara E Martin

Haiku

Little birds singing,
Waiting for me to feed them,
Teaching us to hope.

A young boy's body
Riddled with cruel bullets.
What wrong had he done?

Grass like a meadow,
Daisies and dandelions rife.
Get out my mower!

Pleione Tooley

Let's Raise A Cheer
(To the tune of 'Beer, Beer, Glorious Beer!')

Cheers! Cheers! Let's raise a cheer
For all the runners who're here!
They've run the Marathon
Till all their strength has gone
Coming from towns far and near!
To London Town they've come,
From other lands come some,
Dressed in most outlandish gear!
Money they've raised this day
For charities to pay.
Hip! Hip! Hip! Hip! Hip! Hooray!

    Roma Davies

Sam

Slit-eyed, sleepy Sam
Stirs, stretching silk-furred paws
Luxuriously.

Sam licks his whiskers
Expectantly; meaning,
Where's my saucer of milk?

Chattering briefly,
Twitching, eyelids fluttering,
Sam chases dream-mice.

F Jones

Just Deserts
(To the tune of 'Lille Marlene')

We are going scrumping
Before it is too late
All of us have promised
To meet at the orchard gate.
Silent is our happy throng
As we meander slowly along
Those apples are juicy and delicious
All munch, now stomach ache.

We now are all groaning
And in pain, attempt to flee
The farmer thinks we are poachers
And a great big gun has he.
He fires and misses his targets Phew!
But all that pain flows through and through
As into hives all crashes
Oh Mother, to you we plea.

Caressed and swathed in bandages
A lesson all have learned
Those wretched stings and stomach pains
No more, however hard we yearn.
Soothed by medication puts us right
No more will return to seal our plight
Our thanks to our dear mothers
And of course our loyal, true friends.

R D Hiscoke

Haiku

Midwinter Eve

Star-gleam stares through night,
moon glazes frozen black hills,
cold owls call the hours.

Ageing

Embers burn in clouds,
snow flecks drift from pastel sky.
Old men ponder sleep.

Rebirth

Shoots grin through wet soil,
lilac buds entice mischief.
Pretty girls brush hair.

John H Hope

Now They're Teetotelin (Based On True Events)
(To the tune of 'Waltzing Matilda')

Once the jolly Fewtrells camped for tin to mine
Strewth, the mine caved in, causing twins to flee,
So they waltzed to a shack on Croun land, suited fine and
Now they're teetotelin and live heartily.

Now they're teetotelin
Now they're teetotelin
Now they're teetotelin, pensioners - Aussie
And the bush seeps more and more
Into George and Billy's bones and
They never miss a film 'bout 'Crocodile Dundee'.

   R Wiltshire

Example Of Haiku

Morning

Morning is born grey
Mother Sun gives him colour
The wind is his breath.

Kathleen

My shadows of gloom
dispel in the shining glow
of your loving smile

Autumn

Leaves fall silently
The old year has begun to die
The tears of nature.

Neil A Forrester

Untitled
(To the tune 'She Was A Sweet Little Dickie Bird')

Most of the people who visit me, are good friends you see,
Coming to cheer me up, spending the time happily.
They go back home, leaving memories fond and rare,
Otherwise life would be so dull, they put the sunshine there.

Some relate happenings they have shared, making eyes open wide,
Seeing through yarns they tell what life is like outside,
In our heads we see pictures of times today,
Those our living storybooks, we want to read each day.

Small cakes they bring which their hands have made,
                                        sweet as sweet they be.
We enjoy eating them over a cup of tea.
Knit or sew or maybe just chat each day,
This is life's special gift to folk, as the years tick away.

    Barbara Goode

Haiku

Changing Faces

Sunshine deserts walls;
leaving winter to apply
a green overcoat.

No Flow

The gentle slap, slap,
of water on stone has ceased;
high tide hesitates.

Two Ways To Go

Worms stir hallowed ground;
autumn anticipation
cremation denies.

S R Green

Salome's Request Granted
(Sung to the tune about a German Ace Pilot)

The young girl, aged fifteen, very attractive,
Make-up around the eyes,
Smoothed on from blue iris,
Growing along the banks of the River Nile.
The king wondered what her request would be
When the Dance of Honour ended.
His queen, mother of his stepdaughter,
Had earlier said what to ask for.
The music stopped,
Applause was loud.
'Now what would you like?' the king said to Salome.
Bowing before him she said
'Bring me the head of John The Baptist on a silver salver.'
She knew that her mother did not like the preaching by him.
Astonished, the request of Salome was granted by the king.

Marguerite A Auton

Birth

A gentle thump, thump,
that's all I hear, but very
comforting, thump, thump.

A hard push, it comes
again, that's all I feel; not
very comfy now.

Cut me free, snip, snip,
The noise! The light! Let me breathe.
Snip, snip. I've been born.

Sue Colson

Haiku

Lost Illusions

Fluffy cotton cloud,
Slanting evanescent trail:
Glinting metal shroud.

Statue In Winter

Bronze in crystal net:
Hoar frost chills love's ecstasy
Till Spring brings freedom.

Brother

Tickles yield chuckles.
Boy clambers, laughing and hugs
Baby and mother.

    Frances Searle

Woke Up This Morning With Ye Larke
(To the tune of 'In Good King Charles' Golden Day')

Woke up this morning with ye larke
I do not know where it came from
It was not there when one went to bed
After eating one's onion and bacon.

Got up with ye larke
It did not do one much good
It did not make one any forrader
For one sat and one scratched
For a full two houre
Then one went and raided ye larder.

Went in ye bedroom
To put on one's clothes
One did not draw ye curtain
For *no* bodie went by at that hour
Of this one was quite certain.

Well on this occasion some bodie did
It was one early postie
He looked in ye window, flipped ye lid
And turned as pale as a ghostie.

Well alack and ado
What a naughtie thing to do
He went and told the nation
And now to put ye lid on it
He's claiming compensation.

Well alack and ado
What is one supposed to do?
One has to put one's bra on
For to lift up ye boobs, for if one do not
There is a chance they will get sat on.

Well alack and ado
What a fine how do ye do?
I hope ye will be sympathetique
For if ye be not, I think that one
May have to go peripatetique.

Norah Morley-Koyich

My Song
(To the tune 'The Londonderry Air')

I'll sing a song to a lovely piece of music, in a street in Limavady town
There on a house, a plaque is to record it,
Where Jane Ross wrote this music down,
She heard a travelling minstrel play it, on the street below her home,
He had no script for it, but from memory played it,
As on the roads he would daily roam.

It was from his father he had learned it, just handed down from
                                                     father unto son.
In Jane's drawing room, he played it over,
And so its preservation was begun.
A music teacher, she knew how to do it,
And carefully she wrote it there
And for posterity she then entitled it 'The Londonderry Air'.

Nan W Downs

Haiku

Celebrate in style
The Queen's Golden Jubilee
All around the world.

Narrow canal boat
Floats in a watery scene
Peaceful and tranquil.

Duck dips in water
Shower fountain all around
To cool in the heat.

    Sylvia Berwick

Wouldn't Start
(To the tune 'Wooden Heart')

Do you know I've phoned you
'Cause my car key's broke in two?
What else could I do?
For I don't have a car that'll start.

Would you please, please reply?
And tell me you will try,
I know that I will cry,
If I don't get my car to start.

There's no life in this old car of mine,
'Twas always good for me to start,
Treat it nice, treat it good,
Just like a surgeon would.
Please make the new key good,
For I do need a car that'll start.

Wenn The Penn

Haiku

Stitch In Time

Winter memories
knit one, purl one, saving thoughts.
A patchwork of dreams.

The Duck

Surrounded by swans
he struts to defend his patch.
Alas . . . bowled for nought!

The Fall

Sombre irony
twin towers formed eleven.
Their last autumn morn.

    Elizabeth Wilson

Super Bob Taylor
(To the tune 'Davy Crockett')

He was born in a castle by a northern town.
A football stronghold of great renown.
His mummy had hoped he would answer the call,
But baby Bob Taylor was hooked on football.
He practised daily with a toilet roll.
The first words he spoke were, 'I've scored a goal.'
Super Bob, Super Bob,
The would-be football star.

He signed for The Albion on a day of joy,
The team he adored since he was a boy.
When he pulled on the stripes of blue and white,
His heart missed a beat through sheer delight.
Then took the field amidst a thunderous roar,
And walked into fame and footballing lore.
Super Bob, Super Bob,
The pride of The Albion Team.

Battling Bob Taylor had a long-held dream,
To show off his skills against a premier team.
With help from his mates, passion and pride,
Made West Bromwich Albion a premier side.
The strike against Palace was his finest score,
That made him famous for evermore.
Super Bob, Super Bob,
The pride of The Albion Team.

John Hogan

Haiku

Guardsman on duty
Just standing there, motionless,
Gawped at by tourists.

Planning a novel?
Does he hear people talking,
Or has he switched off?

 Kathy Rawstron

I Still Think Of You
(Sung to the tune of 'Love Me Tender')

I still think of you today
Although you're far away
And I wish that you knew
How much that I miss you

But you're gone and you don't know
Just how sad I feel
Knowing that you never cared
Although my love for you was real

And I will still think of you
As the years go by
If only you were here with me
I'd have no need to cry

But you're gone and you don't know
Just how sad I feel
Knowing that you never cared
Although my love for you was real

I wish you would think of me
But I know that will never be
For you never glanced my way
But I think of you each day

But you're gone and you don't know
Just how sad I feel
Knowing that you never cared
Although my love for you was real.

Eileen Kyte

Haikus

The sea is the home
For sardines, herrings and cod,
Nourishment for us.

Restlessly I stirred
Sleep evaded me, I tossed,
Wide-eyed I got up.

The sweet smell of grass
Freshly out in the summer,
It is like perfume.

    Mary Joseph

All For Love
(To the tune of 'Daisy, Daisy, Give Me Your Answer Do'
My father regularly sang it to my mother whose name it was)

Dearest Venus, please will you dance with me?
Gorgeous Venus, come then my partner be.
I know I won't be the greatest:
I could outdo your latest!
Let me entwine
Your arms in mine
And then dance till the dawn we see.

Dearest sweetheart, come to the church with me,
Gorgeous sweetheart, you then my wife to be.
I know my pocket is empty,
But what we'll have in plenty
Is love for you
And me so true
In a marriage of ecstasy.

Owen Edwards

Haiku

Rain kissed rose petals.
Dew drenched the early morning grass.
Sun drank, greedy lips.

Howl wind, roar temper,
Lifting things, discards, vents wrath.
It speeds along paths.

Lonely little bird
Perches high on the steeple
Blowing in the wind.

Angela Henderson

Untitled
(To the tune of 'O My Darling Clementine')

O how vivid - O so vivid
Are the memories of that day
When in smart, new, pleated tunic
I arrived filled with dismay.

O how vivid - O so vivid
Were the memories left behind
Of that dear old school and playmates
Many thoughts were on my mind.

O how vivid - O so vivid
When assembled in the hall
Several hundred brown-clad strangers
Not one face I could recall.

O how vivid - O so vivid
Are those teachers short and tall
Different face for every subject
My old teacher taught them all.

How I missed her, how I missed her
That dear teacher friend of mine
Always giving, always helping
Always cheerful and so kind.

Greta E Bray

Someone Special - Me!

I am mother, wife,
sister, daughter, auntie, niece.
Not yet a grandma.

I am teacher, Miss;
math'matician, organist,
untidy, giving.

I like laughter, hugs,
companionship, recycling,
sunshine, dining out.

I do not like change,
violence, rows, pigs' hearts, queues,
housework, climbing hills.

I hope for friendship,
contentment, knowledge, truth, peace,
common sense and love.

I'm grateful for life;
a loving, growing fam'ly;
caring, sharing friends.

Kathryn M Carter

From Whom No Secrets Are Hid
(To the tune of 'Londonderry Air')

And did you think that you could not be truthful?
And did you think that you would never share?
And did you think that He would not be waiting?
And did you think that He could never care?

Do you not know He's waiting for that 'Sorry'?
Do you not know He's waiting for that sign?
Do you not know He's here to help and heal you?
And do you know, for you, He has the time?

D Howard

Haiku

Fallen autumn leaves
Clothe the earth with red and gold,
Green, they clothed the tree.

Solitary leaf
Swaying in late autumn's breeze;
Remnant of summer.

Pink roses in bloom
On gaunt, naked bare branches,
November bonus.

White frost hides green grass,
Brown trees don a sparkling coat,
On the roads - black ice.

Quick flash of silver
Darts through waving water weeds,
Glimpse of river's wealth.

Meandering stream
Becomes a raging torrent
Swollen with storm rain.

J Buksh

Mum And Dad
(To the tune of 'When I'm Sixty-Four')

As I've grown older, learnt about life,
I know what you've done,
You were always there to wipe my tears away,
You knew what to do and the right things to say,
You taught me what's right and you taught me what's wrong,
You always cared for me,
I am so grateful, eternally grateful, and I'll always be.

I've always felt loved 'cause you've always been there
And this is clear to see,
You showed me how to spell my name and read and write,
You saved me from the monsters in the middle of night,
You've shaped who I am and you've given me strength,
I'm me because of you,
I am so grateful, eternally grateful, for all the things you do.

L Berry

Haikus

A chill in the air
The seasons begin to change
Leaves fall, trees now bare.

The first time you meet,
Eyes drawn across crowded room,
Realise love's a treat.

Life-changing choices,
Leap into maturity,
To be one that wins.

    Louise Lee

Haiku

God, the sun of warmth
Jesus, the dirt of our growth
The Spirit, the rain

Solid rays of sun
Fleeting through the greenery
Mystically gone

Curtain of sun rays
Slanting through the wall of trees
There before, gone now.

John A Mills

A Picnic - Through The Looking Glass
(To the tune of 'The Teddy Bears' Picnic')

If you go down in the woods today
It will take your breath away
Not Goldilocks and the Three Bears
This time, you'll find that there's
One bear and three little girls from school
And what is more you'll find that you'll

Never guess the game they're playing today-ay

Playtime in the woods today
They shuffle, deal and play
And they bid their hearts away
Three no trumps, then double, I say
Good, we've got them, one away
What a lovely game to play
He's trumped my ace - I say, that isn't any fun.

Now we'll have to bid - and make a slam
To make up for that bad one

John the bear and the little girls three
Janette and the two Jeans are we
Bidding on each hand today
Trying for a game to play
A slam would mean we'd have a ball
But you can't win them all if it isn't there

At six o'clock we're off home to bed, three weary little girls
And the tired little teddy bear.

    Joyce Metcalfe

Haikus

Silent hawk hanging
Menacingly motionless
Expecting a kill.

Singer mouth open
Waits gathering the power
To hit the top note.

Comic beseeching
With sad eyes so appealing
Begins his routine.

Jack Scrafton

Make A Change
(To the tune of 'The Greatest Love Of All')

I believe the world could be different
No more worries, no more fighting
No more war or sadness anymore.
Give us the strength to try, to make it easier
Let our smiling faces change the world for evermore.

Everybody needs to join together holding, hand in hand,
To help the children in the world today
This world can be the place where we can all just live as one.

I know we can make it work
All we have to do is help each other
No matter how hard it gets, making a stand for what is best
Because we should start to care for each and everyone
Then we can all be happy
I know that we can
Teaching the children all that's right, to make them achieve

And the world should be a brighter place
Chase away those lonely days, find a time to smile.

Valerie Gaynor

Haiku

Koi carp shimmer in
A garden pool; a passing
Heron takes breakfast.

Friends meet once a year.
Good talk, rich food, too much wine.
Tomorrow - headache.

Crisp golden leaves fall;
A carpet for time shining
On the forest floor.

Emelie Buckner

Words And Music
(To the tune of 'Auld Lang Syne' or 'Sing A Song Of Sixpence')

It will be fun to pen a rhyme
To fit this little song,
With poetic inspiration
To speed each verse along.
To capture words, to contemplate
To focus, then to find,
Lyrics that will linger like
A melody in the mind.

Ideas are now flowing
With excitement on the brink,
While waves of creativity
Converge to make one think.
So to build on the momentum
There is no time to tarry,
Until a blissful state is reached
When words and music marry.

The ballad may not scale the heights
Of Rogers and Hammerstein,
Or ever have a claim to fame
This humble attempt of mine.
Still I have loved this challenge
Of setting words to score,
Now I am very happy to
Hand over - to the Troubadour.

Monica Docherty

Haiku

This is a haiku.
You don't need a high IQ
To pen a haiku.

When studying maps
I travel the whole wide world
In my fireside chair.

It was my first bike;
Passport to the open road;
And sheer happiness.

Alf Godman

Haiku

Lambs bleating on hills
A stream below in the dale
The voice of the moors.

Daffodils in flower
The fields are full of their gold
It's spring in Holland.

Barking in the night
My dog who was lost came home
Please open the door!

M Sleeboom-Derbyshire

Reflections
(To the tune of 'In A Shady Nook')

We know one day we'll see
That true eternity,
Promised to you and me
If we keep true.

All we need is faith
That in a perfect race,
The winners not just one
But multiply.

We can see a future
When all loved ones will be
Gathered unitedly,
Peacefully together.

We know the time will come
For those with faith and love,
For one who reigns above,
Our Heavenly Father.

Yes, one day will be,
For all eternity,
Folk living happily
In a perfect world.

That is your promise true,
For all who follow you,
Jehovah God, above,
And Jesus Christ.

May our love be true
As we follow you
In your paths
Of righteousness.

Then one day we'll see,
For eternity,
Just the way the world
Should be!

Donna Deen

A Woman's Work
(To the tune of 'The Happy Wanderer')

A woman's work is never done,
So people often say,
But as we work from morn till night
We'll keep these thoughts at bay.

We'll work, we'll work, we'll work,
Yes, in our Saviour's precious name
We'll work, we'll work,
We'll work the whole day through.

A Christian's work is never done,
This is the truth you know,
For there are many people who
In Jesus' love don't grow.

So Christian women, we must work
In our dear Saviour's name,
And pray to Him for help each day
For Him more souls to claim.

Anne Gray

Haikus

River Song

Dance with me - River
Act like I do joyfully
Listen be happy.

Gate

Gate full of beauty
God attends to everyone
I'm the gate said He.

Happy

Happy yes or no?
In community who knows
Dance of life in toes.

Bella Carroll

Haiku

The honeybee bumps
against the picture window,
then retreats confused.

The pine drops large cones
into soft snow, making holes
as clues for squirrels.

Children clear the snow
and skate on the pond's thick ice,
laughing and shouting.

Roger Mather

Haiku

Butterfly in flight
On fragile wings colours bright
Of summer petals

Nest hidden in tree
Householder keeping close watch
To protect fledglings.

Freda Grieve

Malfunction
(To the tune of 'The Sunny Side Of The Street')

If you would be my teddy bear,
And show me your charms,
Your stuffing I could prod,
Whilst you were in my arms,

You would reply with a loud growl,
And then your eyes would spin,
Your nose would twitch a lot,
Your face light up with a grin,

Refrain

I would run my fingers through your fur,
And then check all your seams,
When you think the jackpot's near,
I would say 'boy',
Dream on toy,

Then my dress of satin and lace,
I would rearrange once more,
And with my fading batteries,
Head straight for the door.

For I am just a china doll,
Who walks and talks and cries,
Who uses U2 batteries,
Just like the other toys,

And when the action gets too hot,
My batteries 'Ever Ready',
Run right down and stop,
Spoiling things for you teddy,

Refrain

Then lying on the floor,
My eyes are open wide,
There I see Action Man,
And while he's staring,
I'm whirring,

If only they went on and on,
A longer tale I could tell,
Why, oh why, 'Buzz Lightyear',
Was I not fitted with Duracell?

Ann G Wallace

Haiku

The rain is falling
or is it tears in my eyes
since you went away?

Stars shining brightly
lighting the dark blue heavens.
The world seems at peace.

It is good to hear
the birdsong in the morning.
Fills the heart with cheer.

Monica D Buxton

The Unfolding Of Spring
(To the tune of 'All Kinds Of Everything')

Having got through the winter
It's good to see
The leaves unfolding
On flower and tree.
Apple tree, pear tree,
Blossoms awake,
Oh Mother nature,
I think you are great.

Spring is now with us,
Seeds germinate,
To see the seedlings
I can hardly wait.
Primroses, poppies,
Sweet peas too,
All colours of the rainbow
Come into view.

Now for the veggies,
A culinary treat,
Little rows of cabbages
Form at our feet.
Lettuces, radishes,
Spring onions too,
Nice new potatoes
To delight you.

Margaret Kinshott

Haikus

The tiny daisy
Opens its slender petals
In the morning sun.

Delicate snowflake
Landing upon my window
And melting away.

Giant waves crashing,
Splashing upon golden sand.
The sea in a storm.

Kaz

Breakaway Blues
(To the tune of 'Yankee Doodle Dandy')

I was born and bred in London,
Although my heart is never there;
A country-bumpkin lurks within my soul,
I do not need Leicester Square.
If you, perchance, should find me dreaming,
I will be where I belong;
Ploughing fields, or herding cattle,
Riding on a pony;
This is my fantasy in song.

Ducks, and geese, and chickens laying,
Some goats that nibble at my shoes;
For every time I hear old Big Ben's chimes,
I get those breakaway blues.
Content just strolling on the seashore,
Making footprints in the sand;
Building castles, kicking pebbles,
Riding on a pony;
This is the life I understand.

Sunset, moonrise, on the mountains,
The smell of heather in the glen;
My heart is breaking, aching to be free,
Who cares wherever or when.
If you, perhaps, should see me flying,
I am back where I belong;
Chasing rainbows, catching stardust,
Riding on a pony;
This is my fantasy in song.

Mary Halfpenny

Foreshore

Storm

Angry wind and rain,
Storm-lashed beach with broken wood,
This was once a boat.

Shells

Tread carefully now
Shells are sharp - once home to fish
Grind to grains of sand.

Butterfly

The butterfly's wings
Silently still on the earth
Just so - then away.

Maureen Oglesby

Haiku

No sweet song to sing,
Just slight tremble of the wing,
A butterfly lifts.

Crystal clear it hung,
Suspended from a wet lash
Fell a single tear.

Wind flew through the boughs,
Toying with bright pink blossom,
Tossing them in flight.

S Phillips

Haiku

Approaching darkness
Enhancing scenic viewing,
Sunset colouring.

Cascading water,
Spraying, buffeting, swirling,
Enchanting delight.

Blossom appearing.
Colourful, scented, floral,
Covering branches.

B Lamus

The Power Called Love
(To the tune of 'The Power Of Love')

The silence now is broken as lovers wake and sigh,
The darkness of the night has gone as daybreak lights the sky.
I hold her to me closely and feel her warm embrace,
Her voice is soft and gentle,
So full of yearning, I could never resist,
For you are my angel, I'll always be your guy,
Whenever you need me, my love, I'm always nearby.
Sometimes I feel so lonely without you in my arms.
Outside the world seems cold and bare without our love to share,
Although there may be moments you think I've gone away,
Never worry Darling where I am, for I'll be there every day.
For you are my angel, I'll always be your guy.
Whenever you need me, my love, I'm always nearby.
Whatever this feeling, I've never had before.
Sometimes I'm nervous but I'm willing to touch that power
                                          called love.
And as I hold you close to me and I'm the only one
A feeling that my world would ever end if you ever leave me.
For you are my angel, I'll always be your guy,
Whenever you need me, my love, I'm always nearby.
Whatever this feeling I've never had before.
Sometimes I am nervous but I'm willing to touch the power
                                          called love.
Whatever this feeling I've never had before,
Sometimes I am nervous but I'm willing to touch the power
                                          called love,
Oh the power called love, the power called love.
Sometimes I am nervous but I'm will to touch the power
                                          called love,
Oh the power called love, the power called love.

    Tom Usher

Haiku

Going In Style

From a dripping tap
Water drops - going to waste -
Form a diadem.

Marathon

Mind over matter.
One foot before the other.
He won - painfully.

Rainbow

Suddenly the sun
Burst through - raindrops glistened and
A rainbow was born.

Joan Tompkins

Newborn

On the first morning
of the world, honeysuckle
unfurled, towards God.

Tender crocuses
raised frail cups on slender stalks,
seeking the life force.

Imperceptibly,
a breeze rippled new grasses
at Gethsemane.

Our sleeping baby
smiles and, soft as rose petals,
opens his fingers.

Down-slanted breathing
ruffles his crown of peach fuzz:
perfection of form.

Eyelashes like silk
caress his cheeks. His inner
sunlight glows: pure love.

    Faith Bissett

Held So Dear
(To the tune of 'Candle In The Wind')

When sons depart . . .
It's enough to break a mother's heart.

And so it was
On a dismal
Winter's day.

When two cherished ones
In that golden reserve
Of Liverpool's city soul . . .

Her citizens
Had fondly kept,
For different reasons,
Now wept.

Nothing could,
Would,
Or should,
Console.

The news was clear
Pastures new
Beckoned . . .
For two held so dear.

This was supposed to be
A time of coming cheer
And now circumstance
With both of them no longer there
Would force many . . .
A different facial expression to wear.

Goodbye Robbie,
Goodnight George . . .
And God bless you both,
Love, Mother Liverpool.

Malcolm Peter Mansfield

Whatever
(To the tune of 'C'est Magnifique-a')

A Stilton cheese lends pefume to the breeze,
Oo, oo, la, la, c'est magnifique-a.
The maggots too pop up their heads and coo,
'Oo, oo, la, la, c'est magnifique-a.'

With Cheddar try a piece of apple pie,
With Parmesan, some minestrone.
Or you may care for Brie or Camembert,
Or there's that stuff that's green and holey.

The mousetrap sort at Tesco's can be bought,
It's quite their best, nothing could be cheaper.
The mice all croon before they met their doom,
'C'est magnifique-a'.

With Danish Blue, Gruyere and Rochefort too,
The pong' so strong, 'twill make you heave-a,
But should you pale, a whiff of Wensleydale
Will soon restore the joie de vivre-a.

On the rind of Caerphilly you will find
'Land of Our Fathers' written in gold leaf-a.
Yes! Cheese is fine but give me all the wine,
C'est magnifique-a.

Joan Rea

Haiku

Gulled

Screeches on the prom.
I thought two gulls were grounded.
Gulled! Two girls cackled.

Limestone Pavement

To the surface, rock
crusty as Stilton cheese rind
or soda bread, froths.

Silver and Orange

Slivers of silver
slit, sever and rearrange
segments of orange.

Chris Moat

Just One More Blessing
(To the tune of 'O Sole Meo')

Just one more blessing,
      Please give to us.
We ask sincerely,
      Because we must.
We pray each day, Lord, and ask of you,
      Just one more blessing,
To build anew.

To build a new church,
      Is all we ask,
To raise some money,
      To start the task,
It won't be easy, as we all know,
      Just one more blessing
And time will show.

And so we pray, Lord,
      And ask of you,
Just one more blessing,
      To see us through.
As we go forward, our hearts on fire,
      With that one blessing,
We'll never tire.

When we have built it,
      What joy we'll know,
Our work is over,
      But on we'll go.
We'll welcome people from far and near,
      To prove that blessings
Are answered prayer.

    Joan Smith

Haiku

Life

Thrusting, stabbing blade
Fights resistance, pushes up
Green life through parched earth.

Death

Peace at last my friend,
Troubles cease to worry me.
Last breath sighs out life.

Beyond Death

Consciousness expands,
Not life, not death: awareness.
First step without fear.

N D Ifould

Untitled
(To the tune of 'Fight The Good Fight')

Sing together all the time
Sing together with the chime
The seasons come around
With feelings of colour abound
Give with senses all through the year long
Every day the winds of Heaven will sing their song.

S G White

Haiku

The cherry tree blooms
and as the petals descend
the rising sun sets.

I heard a robin
singing from the highest bough
of the tallest tree.

A heap of clothes was
all he left: the rest is best,
in shame, left unsaid.

Joshua Blanchard Lewis

Haiku

The Panda

The panda searches
for bamboo to eat before
his afternoon nap.

The Picnic

Our picnic ended
in chaos when a pony
ate the sandwiches.

The Eclipse

At noon, the moon will
eclipse the sun and the Earth
will be in darkness.

Moon Stone

Untitled
(To the tune of 'The Times They Are A-Changing')

Come all you people throughout the land,
Help each other and give a hand.
You argue the toss, that black is white
And you take to heart the smallest slight,
For the times they are truly amazing.

Oh politicians and generals all,
You hear the sound of duty call.
This Pharaisic worldly ball,
You witness it and see it all,
For the times they are truly amazing.

The prostitute and armed robber beget
Jewels for their hair
But they have never met.
The orphan boy weeps in sorrow,
As the child is born on the morrow,
For this world is truly amazing.

I T Hoggan

Haiku

In the water glass
The full moon is shaken by
My first fleeting touch.

The full moon beckons -
The old wolf on the mountain
Howls, with lifted head.

Sheryl Williamson

Dirty White Pickup - The CTRL Test-Pits Song
(To the tune of 'The Ash Grove')

Down yonder green valley, right down to the Medway,
Up yonder bleak hillside, right up to Gravesend,
Where not even Moxies can make any headway,
We're following chainage pegs right round the bend.
Through field and through fly-tip, we seek out our test-pits,
No track too uneven, no field-gate too tight;
Through copse and through hedgerow, though bogs are the best bits,
In a dirty white pickup with a bright orange light.

Our world-famous workmates dig all the Thames shore up,
Run after the Time Team on primetime TV.
The great London Manual is known throughout Europe,
But what are the glories of MoLAS to me?
Now with unprocessed samples our Transit is laden,
We've run out of empty buckets and grid pegs as well.
Can nobody tell me whose budget we're paid on?
Does anyone care about CRTL?

R D Gardner

Haiku

Frothy pink blossoms
waving in the cool spring breeze
soon will fall like tears.

Gold leaves fluttering
in ever-spiralling dance.
Autumn warms my heart.

Jack frost bares his teeth.
Humans wrapped in newspapers.
Where is compassion?

Fuchsia Coles

The Best Of Seasons

Rain now falls gently
Soil welcomes rejuvenation
Plants grow in plenty.

Spring is here at last
Flowers show colours gladly
Now that winter's past.

Soon summer will come
The sun will warm all the land
Proud of its green thumb.

   Meg Phillips

My Home
(To the tune of 'Granny's Highland Hame')

Far away on a hillside a wee village stands
For 'twas built on the side o' a brae.
'Twas there I'd my childhood, and learnt all I know,
And it seems it was just yesterday.
Oh the hills in their grandeur form a girdle all round,
And in winter they're all tipped with snow
'Tis a sight that I long for whenever I'm sad,
For it cheers me and thrills me I know . . .

Chorus

Though I've lived in other places,
It will always be my home.
Though there's not a lot to do,
I visit and I roam,
For Dalry is somewhere special
With memories of my youth.
Oh, to be in old Glenkens . . .
I miss it, that's the truth.

Oh, the church stands so graceful on the banks o' the Ken
Which winds down from Carsfad to Loch Ken.
As kids we went swimming in the river - what fun -
When the turbines came on we'd to run!
And the school, though and old one, was surely the best,
The headmaster respected by all.
Oh, my memories of schooldays and the great times we had,
I hope I will always recall.

Chorus

At the foot of the hill stands the well-used town hall,
As I child I was in it a lot.
There were concerts and flower shows, and dances and films.
You just had to take what you got!

And the shops, they were few, but they catered for you,
For on us did their wages depend,
But all cared for each other and did what we could.
If in trouble, a hand we would lend.

Chorus

Mary McLeod

The Irish Sing-Along
(To the tune of 'When Irish Eyes Are Smiling')

There is a place in Ireland, a welcome there will be
After travelling many miles, across the Irish Sea
When you pack your troubles in your old suitcase
A greeting is a-waiting, and many a friendly face

It may be early dawn, or through the evening light
When the moon shines o'er the city and stars, are shining bright
A piano will be playing, as we all sing along
As we know the chorus, to this merry old song

All those troubles, and worries, are all kept at bay
As we dance, through the night, till the break of day
Dublin is the city, where we all need to go
Cos, they all know how to party, and go with the flow.

Jean P McGovern

Haiku

Soft light weaves magic
As dawn seeps across the moors
Like the melting snow.

No time to waste friends,
Beaujolais tasting awaits
Hurry, through the gates!

Aloha, dear friend
Your broken heart I'm here to
Ease with thought and deed!

Sarah Allison

Distraction
(To the tune of 'The Ballad Of Barbara Allen')

I've set myself a task today.
I want to write a poem,
A sonnet or a villanelle:
More likely awful dogg'rel.

Should it rhyme or be blank verse?
What should the metric count be?
Didactic or satirical,
Or simply sentimental?

I really cannot concentrate!
A tune my mind invading,
Is slowly sending me quite mad,
It's some old country ballad.

Pamela Sanders

Haiku

Progress

Today a river,
Yesterday, a drop of rain.
Tomorrow, an ocean.

Contentment

Like gentle breezes,
Contentment comes quietly
Silent and soothing.

Serenity

Lightning precedes
Thunder and torrential rain.
Cool breezes follow.

Jean Rosemary Regan

Help
(To the tune of 'My Love Is Like A Red, Red Rose')

Dear God I ask please walk with me
Along life's thorny path
And give to me your help and strength
To face the future's wrath
For I have loved thee all my life
Even tho' sometimes did stray
I've always tried to live your word
Please hear my prayer today.

Storm clouds they gather in the air
Soon tears like rain downpour
Please take my hand and lead me thro'
The darkest of all hours
Please make me strong that I may bear
This heavy-hearted chore
And bring me and my family
Safely to the shore.

Many no doubt have also walked
Along this self-same scree
And sought an answer from you Lord
Why do ye this to me?
I must believe you have a plan
Within which all must fall
Please help me to retain my faith
'Til I too get your call.

Amen.

    Archie Livingstone

Japanese Haiku

Winter brings rest time.
Warmly wrapped lie bud and beast
waiting spring's fanfare.

A dewdrop lies hid
in the heart of a rosebud.
Move gently, brown bee.

Where we used to play,
children no longer scramble.
Death lies around them.

Kathleen M Hatton

A Pig's Tale
(To the tune of 'Please Release Me')

Please release me, let me go
I'm just a baby lamb, you know
I don't want to go with you
Release me, don't turn me into stew

I just want to have a life
Grow up, get wed and have a wife
So please, I beg you let me go
Release me, don't kill me, oh please no

I'll be good, I'll go to school
I'll even let you have my wool
If only you will spare my life
Release me, don't cut me with your knife

I was painted 107
And now I'm sitting here in Heaven
I was killed and eaten quick
I'm laughing because I made you sick!

  H Phillips

Floral Tributes

Violet so shy
Why hide your presence from me
You I would espy

Rose so beautiful
I cherish your loveliness
Content to admire

Hyacinth holds sway
Your looks, your colour, your scent
Intoxicate me.

Beryl Johnson

Shady Stan
(To the tune of 'The Real Slim Shady')

Whatever you think of him
He's your biggest fan
He's so sick and tired of being admired
Stations won't play his scam-jam
Critics can't stomach it
Everyone needs to relax
Stand up, shout loud
I am, I am Shady Stan Stan
Shady Stan, that's oh me, the man
We all have issues
So mad or just cute so
Everyone has opinions
Discs are mad, bad, even sad
Why don't we relax
Stop hitting back
Give some slack with the chat
It was you and only you
Your biggest fan, Shady Stan.

E A Triggs

Flowering Haiku

Feel the warm pleasure
Of English sun in springtime
Take time for leisure.

Sun breaks through again
Brighter than before perhaps
Following the rain.

After winter's hold
Now we are free to wander
Without feeling cold.

Barbara Fosh

Parody On Goodbye
(To the tune of 'The White Horse Inn')

My heart is broken, oh why, oh why?
My love lives over the ocean,
Now far away, I am lonely today
And ne'er can a word be spoken.
I love her madly, I wish she'd stay.
Her photo she left as a token.
Now feeling blue, what can I do?
My door I will ever leave open.
I'm not happy, she's not happy,
All our friends are most unhappy.
Lord bring my loved one to me;
Tell her I love her, waiting just to be with her,
To my heart, she has the key;
Please end my heartbreak, send her to me,
Or take me to her, to happy be;
Though far away, I would get there some way
Just tell me she really needs me.
Goodbye my friends, I must away to be with Anne.
Goodbye my blues, I'll be a very different man.
Laughing, singing, walking in the rain,
I'll bid all my troubles goodbye
Once I put my arms around my sweetheart again,
I'll throw my hat in the sky.
Goodbye, I wish the world goodbye,
Goodbye, and *hello to Anne and I.*

Lionel J Nokes

Haiku

Drooping daffodils,
golden blooms of yesterday.
Come back, beloved.

Look before you leap.
Sage advice to all the young
except Columbus.

The white grubs panic.
A robin swoops, their gunship
on freshly dug earth.

Tony Meaney

The White Cliffs Of Dover
(To the tune of 'The White Cliffs Of Dover')

When the day is over
And sleep befalls us
Tomorrow comes a brand new day.

There'll be work and laughter
With friends and others
And time to enjoy a cup of tea.

A time to enjoy
What the day brings that's good,
A time to reflect
On the way we behaved.

When the day is over
And sleep befalls us
Tomorrow comes a brand new day.

Clare Collins

Haiku

The roar of the sea,
mighty waves of Burry Holms
as the storm clouds come.

The iridescent
water changes from golden
as the sky turns black.

Ghost memories flash
But the waves still slash the rocks
On wild Burry Holms.

Guy Fletcher

Hay Fever
(To the tune of 'You Go To My Head')

You go to my chest, where you linger like an unwanted guest,
Causing outbreaks that disfigure my vest -
Freckly rashes make me awfully depressed.

You go to my nose, as last summer when romancing in Spain,
Sinusitis blocked me up like a drain
And I couldn't tell Seven-Up from champagne.

Though without belief in obtaining relief -
Poor lover, I'm destined to suffer -
Still it's one of my tricks to pack menthol and Vicks
And balm in the shape of my puffer.

You go to my head since hay fever makes my temp'rature rise -
When the brochure writes of 'sheer paradise',
Very frequently my will to live dies.

Bitter sweet, this condition of mine -
My medical plans confounding my dreams of romance.
You go to my chest.

Norman Bissett

Untitled

Pearls strung on a twig
decorating bare tree with
necklace of raindrops.

Behind black mountains
vast red splashes disappear
as sun lowly sets.

Sending forth flashes
on bright shimmering water
golden sunlight gleams.

Beryl Adamsbaum

Shanty In Old Shanty Town
(To the tune of 'Shanty In Old Shanty Town')

It's just a little fleapit that's no bigger than a larder
A Fridgidare . . . a life-sized print of Lollobrigida's father,
A small place at the back, big enough to hang your hat in
A length of chain, a noisy drain . . . a yard of coconut matting.

It's got a Hotpoint and a telly, the lighting is diffused
A rumbleseat, a place for meat and a cat that's been misused
And the reason why I'm not there now, and sing so mournfully,
Is there isn't any room there for that great fat blonde and me!

Lincoln Allen

Summer Haiku

Aeroplane droning
leaves behind a white scribble
for the birds to read.

Jingle – ice cream van -
children appear from nowhere,
wafers, cornets drip.

Summer whispering
among the leaves of all trees
that hide in cool places.

Chris Creedon

Young Swinger
(To the tune of 'Soul Singer')

I am a younger swinger looking for some fun
Here tonight that has just begun
All I need is someone to love
Just for tonight is good enough
Young swinger, yes young swinger.

I am a young swinger looking for some fun
In a pub, a club, maybe your house
Yet where I shall sleep there is some doubt
Maybe with a down-and-out
Young swinger, yes young swinger.

I am a young swinger looking for some fun
Hey my life has only just begun.
So let us swing away while the night is young
In to some love we can make fun
Young swinger, yes young swinger.

Keith L Powell

Loving Lord Jesus
(To the tune of 'Bunessan' - 'Morning Has Broken')

Loving Lord Jesus, gentle but powerful,
Showed His compassion when on this Earth.
Blind, lame and lepers, those who had demons
Healed through His power, blessed by His birth.

Healing and wholeness Christ still delivers,
Meeting each person at point of need.
Healing the broken, healing the spirit,
Showing God's goodness by word and deed.

Hands that are God's hands healing His people,
Used by His faithful in Jesu's name.
Asking in prayer for Christ's intervention,
His mercy flowing through hands again.

Loving Lord Jesus, gentle but powerful;
Still shows compassion to us on Earth.
Healing divisions, comforting sadness,
Healed through His power, blessed by His birth.

Dennis Brockelbank

Untitled
(To the tune of 'Beautiful Dreamer')

Beautiful dreamer open your eyes
I know what you told me wasn't all lies
You are my sweet love, my innocent dove
Beautiful dreamer please waken my love

When the officer told me that you nearly died
I had to be with you, I swallowed my pride
I'm here with you Darling, stroking your head,
I'll never forsake you, I'll sit by your bed

I beg you my sweetheart don't die on me
Give us some time to plan our own family
A girl that is blonde with blue eyes just like you
A boy that is rugged and plays football too

Beautiful dreamer I'm holding your hand
Give me a sign that you understand
If you can hear me grip my hand tight
Give me some hope that you'll be alright

Beautiful dreamer open your eyes, give
Me a smile and a wondrous surprise
Don't ever leave me, come back to life
I'll love you forever my beautiful wife

When you awaken, I'll be waiting here
Even if you don't wake up for a year
If the time comes when we have to part
You'll always be with me here in my heart.

A Whyte

Haiku

Daffodils

As clouds sail away
Daffodils shine at the sun.
Suddenly it's spring.

Cherry Blossom

White cherry blossom
Showers my path with fragrance
And fragile beauty.

Butterflies

Amongst the bracken
Flashes of butterfly wings
Flit, then dip from view.

Anne Greenhow

Golden Jubilee
(To the tune of 'Dead Wood Stage' from 'Annie Get Your Gun')

Oh the jubilee is a'coming around this year,
Oh the jubilee is a'coming around this year,
Nothing can ever bring her down,
Glorious crown, glorious crown, glorious crown.

'Tis fifty years since the crown sat on her head,
'Tis fifty years since the crown sat on her head,
'Long may she reign,' the whole country said.
Crown on her head, crown on her head, crown on her head.

Queen Elizabeth II will be known,
Queen Elizabeth II will be known,
Ruling with grace and high dignity,
Long live she, long live she, long live she.

Oh the banners are hanging in the streets ye know,
Oh the banners are hanging in the streets ye know,
Let's raise our hands and cheer as she goes,
Bow our heads low, bow our heads low, bow our heads low.

Oh the jubilee is a'coming around this year,
Oh the jubilee is a'coming around this year,
Nothing can ever bring her down,
Glorious crown, glorious crown, glorious crown.

Susan Sissons

Haiku

Sunshine through showers
Brings brightly-coloured rainbows,
Lighting dark corners.

A smile costs nothing,
But like a ray of sunshine
Brightens up your day.

Dancing in the sun,
Butterflies on buddleia
Perform their ballet.

Angela Pritchard

Among Our Souvenirs
(To the tune of 'Among My Souvenirs')

Our weight we have to watch
Else Agnes will be cross
She says now I'm the boss while you're with me
Her skinny legs she shows
She's slim from head to toes
And wears size 12 in clothes, now we can be the same
So we must exercise
And lose weight from our thighs
We really should be wise and cut down on our intake
When all is said and done
Weight Watchers is the one
So we can put that ton among our souvenirs

Sarah Buchan Anderson

Along The Grantham Canal

Across the cornfields
hedges and trees, image sharp
3d'd by bright sun.

Amongst the hawthorn
early August blackberries
surprise chance bramblers.

Stop, start dragonflies
helicopter the canal
in perfect silence.

R L Cooper

Drink To Me Only
(Words by Ben Johnson 1574-1637)

Drink to me only with thine eyes
And I'll pledge thee in red wine,
Or leave a kiss within the cup
And I will sup on the red stuff;
And thirst that from the bubbles rise
Will make me want enough and enough.
And more, oh drink to me only
In wine full ruddy and I'll write
In praise of your bloody eyes
Appearing over the cup
Ben you surely meant not this.
Thy thirst did playfully arise
From the soul; mine seeks a kiss,
A joy less wholesome.
Come, bite your lip in wild desire
And I will taste the blood
That comes from thee to me.
I from such nectar shrink not;
In that red vein I'll surely drink
Bacchic joys most divine.
Nought would I change for blood
Of thine when you to me
Can promise this . . . rare felicity.
Am I as pagan as Keats in his ode?
Is chalice of mine by
Gods of old refined? No, for I go
With sensual dreams along.
Of pillaged bodies is my song;
Spare me your purity
And then I'll drink to thee,
But only in red wine.

    John K Coleridge

Haiku

A single tear falls
Mixes eye shadow with rouge
In a colour box.

Blue swallow dips, plucks
Mosquito on the water.
Fly past for summer!

An empty pistol,
Blood upon the crisp white snow.
Love's scenario!

Michael Monaghan

Now
(To the tune of 'Under The Bridges Of Paris')

Now that the sun is up
Now that the sky is blue
Now that I'm loving you
Can it really be true?
Waiting, it took so long I know
I had to be strong
Now at last I belong to you.

Bernadette Leary

Haiku

Autumn's perfect rose
Sits in the garden's glory
While all others fade.

White blossom falls down
Just like snowflakes from the tree,
Is this spring I see?

Beautiful sunshine
As the bird rests, eating grain,
Wind puffs the cobwebs.

    Elizabeth Ellis

Wok Of Ages
(To the tune of 'Rock Of Ages')

Wok of China cook for me
A Chinese meal for my tea.
Sweet and sour chicken would be nice
Especially with some egg fried rice.

Stir fry eggs with tomatoes
Are really good as good food goes,
Lamb with mushrooms and bamboo shoots
For meals like this I'd sell my boots.

For dessert: apple fritters, mandarin style
Or banana fritters would make me smile
It would be really nice if you could make
A lovely, fluffy, steamed Cantonese cake.

All these lovely wholesome recipes
How nice it must be to be Chinese
But I am English, and as English goes
It'll be roast beef with potatoes!

T W Denis Constance

Haiku

Pleasure

A birthday present
Wrapped in a special paper,
What a nice surprise!

Decision

She paused on the step,
Would she jump, or would she not?
She decided not!

Hope

We are striving for
Pleasure each day of our lives,
But seldom get it.

    Mary McPhee

Realism

Accents are nothing
When words are choicely spoken
With a kindly voice

A pleasant manner
That makes this life worth living
Is judged by the thought

Beautiful creature
Is the stag, infinite, proud,
Monarch of nature.

Beatrice Newman

Haiku

One day, the sunset
Will happen for the last time.
So cherish today's . . .

As the leaf floats down,
I alone of all mankind,
Will have seen it fall.

These rocks were ancient,
When dinosaurs stepped on them.
I can't take that in!

    Frank Casey

Sometimes When We Touch
(To the tune of 'Sometimes When We Touch')

You ask me if I love you
And I choke on my meat pie
I'd rather hit you with a frying pan
Than look you in the eye
And who am I to judge you
When you wobble down the stair,
With your stinking feet,
Your yellow teeth
And your mop of matted hair?

Chorus

And sometimes when we touch
The disappointment is too much
And I have to run away and hide.
You won't eat unless it's fried
I wanna hit you till you've died
I wanna hit you till the fear of you subsides.

You said that if I loved you
Then your size shouldn't matter
I sent you flowers and bought you gifts
But you just got blooming fatter.
Our wedding day was wonderful
You looked so slim and neat
But since you started on the wedding cake
All you've done is eat.

And sometimes when we touch
The disappointment is too much
And I have to run away and hide.
You won't eat unless it's fried
I wanna hit you till you've died
I wanna hit you till the fear of you subsides.

Link

Emotionally blackmailed and dragged around Tesco's aisles,
You wanted me to make love after saying you had piles.

And sometimes when we touch,
The disappointment is too much
And I have to run away and hide.
You won't eat unless it's fried
I wanna hit you till you've died
I wanna hit you till the fear of you subsides.

J Baird

Haikus

Darkness defeats light
the shadow man creeps over
everything is sound.

Clear blue, pure waters,
winding round a river bend
flowing forever.

Laughter is magic,
the only cure to sadness.
Laughter creates love.

Charlene Soan

Haiku

Three-score years and ten,
Septuagenarian,
Am I near the end?

The clock ticks away,
Let time be irrelevant,
Live life to the full.

The heart's pacemaker
Regulates the beating heart,
Until you break it.

Kath Gabbitas

Haiku

People are as leaves
Everyone is different
Not one is the same.

Life is God's garden
Where all mankind is in bloom
Part of God's harvest.

In the garden's peace
Happy is the poet's heart
As he paints with words.

Peter Morriss

Haiku

Only the ivy
With tenacious strength supports
The slow dying bricks.

Forsythia bursts
Round lambs on flash-flood islands
After the fierce storm.

My fine Maygold rose
Snuffs out politicians
Of all other shades.

    Olwen Way

Haiku

Old starlight comes here,
Bearing news from far in haste.
Ah! Someone has seen!

Mere molecules merged.
Lightning flicked atoms around.
This chaos hatched life.

Last year's dead things rot,
Refreshing the worm-tilled soil.
Then Spring comes once more.

David Bowers

Haiku

A Terrible Grief

My healthy son just
Died quite unexpectedly!
Tears have not yet come.

No Climate - Just Weather

The spring came early,
Sunny days but freezing nights.
Beware nesting birds!

Many Against One

Hunting's called a sport!
But only the huntsmen win.
Ban such cruelty.

Marcelle Williams

Haiku

Welcome small stranger
Greetings wondrous little boy
Thank you for our joy.

Golden summer days
For us to play in the sand
All at your command.

William Dyer

Haiku

The stranger steps back
To frame both ruddy children
And beaming parents.

A single sparrow
Revisited the table,
Months after her death.

Obediently
He turns to fetch a size 12;
The assistant smirks.

Andrew Detheridge